Susan B. Anthony

by Lucia Raatma

Compass Point Early Biographies

Content Adviser: Professor Sherry L. Field,
Department of Social Science Education, College of Education,
The University of Georgia

Reading Adviser: Dr. Linda D. Labbo,
Department of Reading Education, College of Education,
The University of Georgia

COMPASS POINT BOOKS

Minneapolis, Minnesota

FLINT RIVER REGIONAL LIBRARY

Compass Point Books
3722 West 50th Street, #115
Minneapolis, MN 55410

Visit Compass Point Books on the Internet at *www.compasspointbooks.com* or e-mail your
request to *custserv@compasspointbooks.com*

Photographs ©:

University of Rochester Library, cover; Stockbyte, cover; Archive Photos, 4, 6 (top), 10, 12 (top), 24 (top); North Wind
Picture Archives, 6 (bottom), 12 (bottom), 13; Library of Congress, 7, 16, 19, 21, 24 (top); Hulton Getty/Archive Photos,
8 (top and bottom), 9, 14, 15, 17, 18, 24 (bottom); Library of Congress, Bettman/Corbis, 20, 25; Unicorn Stock Photos/
David P. Dill, 26.

Editors: E. Russell Primm and Emily J. Dolbear
Photo Researcher: Svetlana Zhurkina
Photo Selector: Linda S. Koutris
Designer: Bradfordesign, Inc.

Library of Congress Cataloging-in-Publication Data

Raatma, Lucia.
    Susan B. Anthony / by Lucia Raatma.
        p. cm. — (Compass Point early biographies)
    Includes bibliographical references and index.
    ISBN 0-7565-0069-9
        1. Anthony, Susan B. (Susan Brownell), 1820–1906—Juvenile literature. 2. Feminists—
United States—Biography—Juvenile literature. 3. Suffragists—United States—Biography—
Juvenile literature. 4. Women social reformers—United States—Biography—Juvenile literature.
[1. Anthony, Susan B. (Susan Brownell), 1820–1906. 2. Suffragists. 3. Women—Biography.]
I. Title. II. Series.
    HQ1413.A55 R33 2001
    324.6'23'092—dc21   00-010938

Table of Contents

Working for a Better World

Susan B. Anthony was a brave woman. She worked for equal rights for all people. She fought for women's rights. She also fought for the rights of African-Americans. She worked to make schools better. And she tried to make workplaces safer. Her story is one of courage and strong will.

◀ Susan B. Anthony

Life in Massachusetts

Susan Brownell Anthony was born on February 15, 1820. She and her family lived in Adams, Massachusetts. They were members of the Quaker Church. Quakers believe strongly in fairness and peace. The Anthonys were **devout** Quakers.

Susan and her family were Quakers.

◀ Susan lived with her family in Adams, Massachusetts.

A Move to New York

Rochester, New York, in the mid-1800s

The Anthony family moved to Rochester, New York, when Susan was twenty-five. Many Americans had slaves during this time. The Anthony family worked hard to stop slavery. Slaves were owned by their masters and were not paid for their work. Most were treated badly. Most slaves were African-Americans. They worked on **plantations** in the South.

The Nation Divided

Slaves being moved south from Richmond, Virginia, after being sold

Slavery was a big problem in the United States. Most people in Northern states were against it. And most people in Southern states thought it was good. They needed slaves to work on their plantations. Slavery was one of the issues that started the Civil War (1861–1865).

Many groups in the North, like this one in Ohio, worked to end slavery.

Susan and her family held meetings to protest against slavery. Susan worked hard to end slavery. She made speeches and put up posters. Many people were angry about her work. Some even threatened to kill her. But Susan Anthony never gave up. She always worked for what she thought was right.

◄ The American Civil War was fought in part over the issue of slavery.

An Important New Friend

In 1851, Susan met Elizabeth Cady Stanton. Stanton worked for women's rights. The two women began to work together. They shared many interests. Their work helped to end slavery. They also worked to give African-Americans the right to vote.

◀ Elizabeth Cady Stanton

Working for Better Schools

Susan began working as a teacher at an early age. She found many things in schools that needed to be corrected. She saw that women teachers were paid less than men teachers. She saw that

Anthony believed that schools needed to be improved.

boys often got better educations than girls.

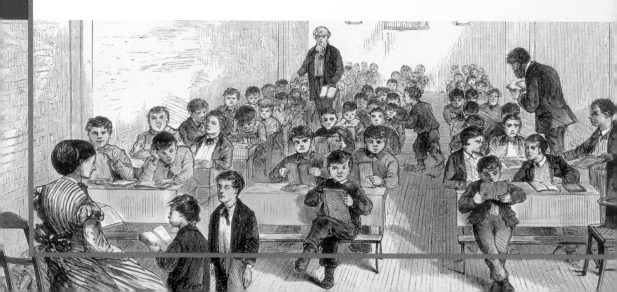

Susan spoke out about these problems. She made speeches at **conventions** of teachers. She demanded better pay for women. She pointed out that women were

Anthony spoke out about the problems in America's schools.

as smart as men. She also wanted freed slaves and their children to be allowed to go to school.

◄ Anthony taught school from an early age.

A Newspaper Is Born

Susan began publishing her own newspaper when she was forty-eight. It was called *The Revolution*. Susan wrote articles about the problems that many workers faced. At this time, many people worked for ten or twelve hours a day. Even young children worked. Also,

Anthony was very concerned about child labor.

children and women were not paid as much as men were. Susan tried to make workdays shorter and to make pay more equal.

The Temperance Movement

Another cause Anthony worked for was **temperance**. Temperance means not drinking alcohol at all, or drinking just a small amount. As a Quaker, Susan grew up believing that drinking alcohol was wrong. As an adult, she saw the problems that alcohol could cause. Many families were in trouble because the parents were drinking too much. She felt that laws about alcohol should be stronger.

Anthony spoke out against alcohol because she knew it could ruin family life.

Elizabeth Cady Stanton helped Anthony with her temperance work. The two women asked the government to pass stricter laws. But the lawmakers did not listen to the women. At that point, Anthony and Stanton knew that women must get the right to vote. Women would have the power to change things only if they could vote.

A Woman's Right to Vote

At this time in the United States, many people believed that women should stay out of politics. Some people believed that women could not think as well as men! But women finally began to argue that they were just as smart as men were.

Only men could be elected to the U.S. Congress during Anthony's time.

◀ Stanton and Anthony formed a group to work with the government to pass better laws about alcohol.

When Susan and Elizabeth had worked to end slavery, they thought that rights for women would also get better. But they were disappointed. Even after African-American men were allowed to vote, women were not. Susan knew that her next goal had to be woman **suffrage**—the right to vote.

African-American men could vote, but women could not.

In 1849, Susan and Elizabeth formed another group. This group traveled from state to state. It worked hard to get women the right to vote. In 1869, Wyoming became the first state that allowed women to vote. Susan Anthony was forty-nine years old.

Wyoming was the first state to give women the right to vote.

Speaking and Risking Arrest

In the years that followed, Susan Anthony spoke all over the United States. In 1872, she was arrested for voting in New York. She was taken to jail but then released on bail. At her trial, the judge found her guilty and told her to pay $100. She refused to pay the fine.

Anthony regularly spoke to congressmen about giving women the right to vote.

Susan Anthony spoke to the members of Congress about woman suffrage. She spoke in Congress every year from 1869 to 1906. She never gave up. Even when the lawmakers would not listen to her, Susan Anthony kept speaking out. It must have been hard to keep going. But Susan never let herself give up.

Women who tried to vote were arrested.

Anthony's Later Years

Throughout her life, Susan also worked for other, more personal, rights for women. Women were often treated badly during the early 1800s. Men were in charge of everything. Women had to do as they were told. Susan knew that things needed to change. She believed women should be allowed to own property. She felt women should be able to have money of their own. And she thought women should have a more equal role in marriage.

Anthony believed that women should be able to own property and have money of their own.

This class of women graduates from Barnard College in New York City, 1901, was among the first in the United States.

Even as she grew older, Susan Anthony never slowed down. In her seventies, she worked to have women admitted to the University of Rochester. Women first attended that college in 1900.

An original copy of the ▶
Nineteenth Amendment

BAINBRIDGE COLBY,
Secretary of State of the United States of America.

TO ALL TO WHOM THESE PRESENTS SHALL COME, GREETING:

KNOW YE, That the Congress of the United States
the first session, sixty-sixth Congress begun at Was
on the nineteenth day of May in the year one thousand
hundred and nineteen, passed a Resolution as follows
to wit-

JOINT RESOLUTION
Proposing an amendment to the Constitution extending
right of suffrage to women.

Resolved by the Senate and House of Representat
of the United States of America in Congress assembled
(two-thirds of each House concurring therein), That t
following article is proposed as an amendment to the
stitution, which shall be valid to all intents and pu
poses as part of the Constitution when ratified by th
legislatures of three-fourths of the several States.

"ARTICLE __.

"The right of citizens of the United States to v
shall not be denied or abridged by the United States
by any State on account of sex.

"Congress shall have power to enforce this artic
by appropriate legislation."

And, further, that it appears from official docu
ments on file in the Department of State that the Ame

In 1906, Susan Anthony died at her home in Rochester, New York. She was eighty-six years old. Fourteen years later, in 1920, the Nineteenth Amendment was added to the U.S. Constitution.

In 1920, women voted for the U.S. president for the first time.

That amendment gave American women the right to vote at last. It was also known as the Susan B. Anthony Amendment.

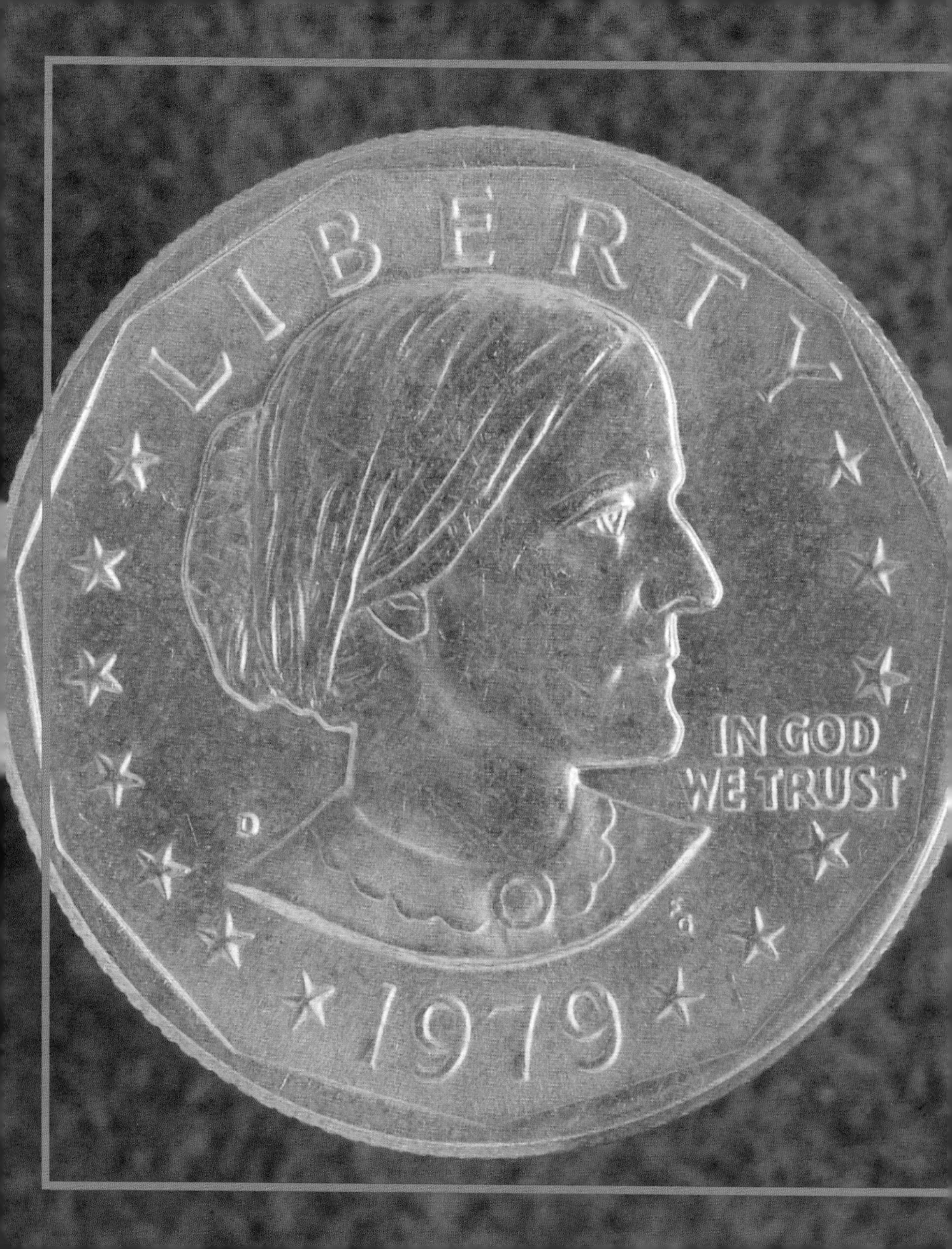
LIBERTY
IN GOD
WE TRUST
1979

A Legend Remembered

Susan Anthony's image was chosen for the dollar coin created in 1979. She was the first woman pictured on U.S. money.

Susan B. Anthony did not live to see some of the success she worked for. But women today are treated better because of her efforts. And all U.S. citizens have equal rights. Her work continues to help people every day.

◄ Anthony was the first woman to be pictured on U.S. money.

Important Dates in Susan B. Anthony's Life

1820	Born on February 15, 1820, in Adams, Massachussetts
1845	Moves with her family to Rochester, New York
1851	Meets Elizabeth Cady Stanton
1868	Begins to edit and publish *The Revolution*
1869	Organizes the National Woman Suffrage Association with Elizabeth Cady Stanton
1872	Is arrested and convicted for voting in a presidential election
1892–1900	Serves as president of the National American Woman Suffrage Association
1906	Dies on March 13

Glossary

conventions—gatherings of people who support similar causes

devout—deeply religious

plantations—large farms, usually in the South, where plants such as cotton are grown

suffrage—the right to vote

temperance—the avoidance of alcohol

Did You Know?

- Susan Anthony was also involved in the fight against slavery.

- When Susan Anthony died, only four states allowed women to vote.

- Susan B. Anthony never married or had children.

Want to Know More?

At the Library

Davis, Lucille. *Susan B. Anthony: A Photo-Illustrated Biography*. Mankato, Minn.:
   Bridgestone Books, 1998.

Parker, Barbara Keevil. *Susan B. Anthony: Daring to Vote*. Brookfield, Conn.:
   Millbrook, 1998.

On the Web

Susan B. Anthony House

http://www.susanbanthonyhouse.org/

For an online tour of Susan B. Anthony's house and other information about her

National Women's Hall of Fame

http://www.greatwomen.org/anthony.htm

For biographical information about Susan B. Anthony

Through the Mail

Chamber of Commerce

55 St. Paul Street

Rochester, NY 14604

For information on sites of interest in Rochester related to Susan B. Anthony's life

On the Road

Susan B. Anthony House

Capital Campaign

17 Madison Street

Rochester, NY 14608

716/235-6124

To visit the house where Susan B. Anthony lived during much of the time she
was active

Index

About the Author
Lucia Raatma received her bachelor's degree in English literature from the University of South Carolina and her master's degree in cinema studies from New York University. She has written a wide range of books for young people. When she is not researching or writing, she enjoys going to movies, playing tennis, and spending time with her husband, daughter, and golden retriever.